T0058016

Also by August Kleinzahler

THE HOTEL ONEIRA

AUGUST KLEINZAHLER

The

HOTEL ONEIRA

———— FARRAR STRAUS GIROUX : NEW YORK ————

FARRAR, STRAUS AND GIROUX

18 West 18th Street, New York 10011

Library of Congress Cataloging-in-Publication Data

Kleinzahler, August.

[Poems. Selections]

The Hotel Oneira / August Kleinzahler. — First edition.

   pages cm

Poems.

ISBN 978-0-374-53481-3

I. Title.

PS3561.L38285 H68 2013

811'.54—dc23

2012049025

Designed by Quemadura

Farrar, Straus and Giroux books may be purchased for
educational, business, or promotional use. For information
on bulk purchases, please contact the Macmillan Corporate
and Premium Sales Department at 1-800-221-7945,
extension 5442, or write to specialmarkets@macmillan.com.

www.fsgbooks.com

www.twitter.com/fsgbooks

www.facebook.com/fsgbooks

P1

. . . all I cared for was the play of words. I would go round savouring a phrase to test it, taste it, till I could decide if it was 'good' or had to be spat out. That word *taste* is not a metaphor. People talk about the sound of language but the real thing is the taste, in the mouth, harsh crisp sweet pungent, produced by the *movement* of sound.

Kenneth Cox

CONTENTS

THE HOTEL ONEIRA

THE HOTEL ONEIRA

That was heavy freight moved through last night,
and has been moving through since I'm back,
settled in again by the Hudson at the Hotel Oneira:
maps on the walls, shelves of blue and white Pelicans,
multiple editions of the one epistolary novel by K.,
the curios—my sediment, you mighty say, my *spattle trail.*

Look at them down there by the ferry slip,
the bridal party, organza, chiffon and lace, beside themselves,
being wonderful, desperately wonderful, a pastel foam.
Behind them a tug pushes a rusted barge upriver.
Helicopters, small planes, passenger jets above.
They behave, these girls, as if this is their last chance to be thus.

You can feel the rumble of the trains
vibrating up the steel of the hotel's frame.
They move only very late at night, from three or so until dawn,
north along the river and then west.

There is going on just now a vast shifting of inventory
from the one place to another. I can feel it, inside my head.

I find myself going down there, late, behind the highway,
at the base of the cliffs, where the track runs.
Last night, what at first looked like a giant coelacanth
strapped to a flatbed rattled slowly past,
but it was merely the enfoldings of a tarp catching the streetlight.
I remember Uncle Istvan at the lake, unaccountably.

This has been going on quite a lot since I'm here.
How is it that I remember him? I saw him but the one time
and was a very small child, at that:
the madras Bermudas, the foreign, almost spastic gestures?
What is in those railcars is also inside my head,
or I imagine it so—no, not imagine, *know*.

How can one know such a thing with certainty? One knows.
Visitors come by my rooms.
The new one, black-haired Ileanna, I most hate to see go.
It is always when the lights first come on across the river,
late in summer, early in winter,
but always when the lights begin over there,
in the countless apartments, with their cloth napkins and vases.

At first, only the late afternoon sunlight,

glinting off windows as the sun lowers in the skies,

but not long after, that's when the lights begin to come on;

that is when she gathers herself and leaves.

There is a story there, but one I choose not to know.

LO MEIN

You were still only a child,
I, nineteen, the age of your eldest boy now.
It was the evening of the Marijuana Caper
your eyes first met mine at the China Chalet.
I believe it would have been spring,
early, but days clearly lengthening,
a patch of ice maybe here or there,
pussy willow catkins . . .
We nearly bought it twice that evening,
my father swerving left and right,
Mother, beside him, silent, stiff with fright.
He was mad at something.
Mad, of course, at life, but mad:
only very occasionally, and on this occasion.
They'd dose a man like that these days,
or try. He'd never have stood for it,
nor any of us, who knew the storm he sailed in
and trembled to be on board with him, but still . . .
Your hair was black, or nearly so,

and long for a child's, partway down your back.
Your eyes dark, as well, roving, restless,
then, as now, taking in the busy room,
as you fitfully dug through your pile of lo mein.
We hadn't planned to get him stoned.
Improvisation was a habit in that household.
He insisted we put it in his pipe,
to prove that he was right, getting high
was humbug, a notion fools entertain.
Mother hid in the kitchen, out of sight.
It was a long-ish drive for us of a Sunday,
but not so long as it ordinarily might have been.
His frenzy, that's what would have caught your eye,
the way he went after it, like a dog at a carcass,
scowling over his left shoulder, then his right,
dare a stranger approach to share or take away
the wonton crisps or dumplings, beef
with scallions, shredded pork, whatever floated by—
New Jersey Chinese fare of the day.
It would have thrilled, or frightened, a child
to behold an adult at table quite so wild.
40 years ago, 40 years . . .
You don't remember all that, do you?
How could you? I'm making it up,
the two of us both there at the same time.

It might easily have been true.
If I made it up it's because it pleases me to.
As you please me, poking through your lo mein,
raising your head nervously to take in the room,
me, and what's doing with the rain.

A HISTORY OF WESTERN MUSIC: CHAPTER 63

(WHITNEY HOUSTON)

They follow you around the store, these power ballads,
you and the women with their shopping carts filled with eggs,
cookies, 90 fl. oz. containers of anti-bacterial dishwashing liquid,
buffeting you sideways like a punishing wind.

You stand, almost hypnotized, at the rosticceria counter
staring at the braised lamb shanks, the patterns
those tiny, coagulated rivulets of fat make,
both knees about to go out from under you.

—Can I help you, sir?
No, no, thank you, I'm afraid not . . .

It's mostly the one woman who writes these things,
a petite, almost perpetually somber brunette

in her L.A. studio, undecorated, two cats,
traffic coursing up and down the boulevard outside,

curtains drawn against the unrelenting sun.
Because of your unconventional lifestyle
you have been shopping among women your entire life,
young mothers and matrons,

almost no other males around except staff and seniors,
the old men squinching their eyes, scowling at the prices.
What sort of life have you led
that you find yourself, an adult male of late middle age,

about to weep among the avocados and citrus fruits
in a vast, overlit room next to a bosomy Cuban grandma
with her sparkly, extravagant eyewear?
It's good that your parents are no longer alive.

It's a simple formula, really: verse, verse, chorus
(and don't take too long to get there),
verse, chorus, bridge, solo, if any,
chorus (good chance of key modulation here—really get 'em),

electric keyboard, soaring guitar, likely a string part or two.
There's no telling how much that woman is worth,

a "misunderstood Jewish girl" from Van Nuys.
How would one go about making love to someone like that,

sitting alone in her studio all day, shades drawn, two cats,
writing these songs of tortured love,
up to the tips of her waders in self-immolation,
often keeping at it well into the night?

Celine Dion, Cher, Michael Bolton, Faith Hill, Toni Braxton—
knocking you back one after another, all morning and afternoon,
at least until the men arrive after work. I don't know why.
Perhaps it has to do with the "emotional nature" of women.

You, you're breathing all funny, nearly paralyzed.
But there's one song they almost never play
and I'll tell you why: it's the one Dolly Parton wrote,
not the brunette, but it's not Dolly who's doing the singing,

it's the one who just died. Because if they played that one,
it wouldn't be just you dying in aisle #5.
All the girls would be dropping like it was sarin gas
pouring from the speakers up there hidden behind the lights.

TUQ-TUQ

Thass me, your jibber-jabbering Sulawesi booted macaque, most
    amused to be
braining rodents with fig buds from up high,
near the tippy-top branch of my tuq-tuq tree, and that's no lie,
when you passed by below wearing I forget now which look.
You gazed up and smiled, sweet-like: "Why not c'mon on down,
    Joe?"
How'd you get on to all that? And we're talking not just "Joe"
but the local macaque lingo? No one else could possibly know
but Mommy Catawba and Sorella-si, who'd prefer not to—know.
So down I scramble, with that studied pause&pose, how I do.
Curious, I was, thrilled, even reckless—given the prospect of jungly
    fare
that might be awaiting me at the bottom there: vipers, crocs, cats—
but careful of my fur, lest the bark catch it up and cause a tear.
Then, *hey presto*, there I y'am, eye to eye with the buckle of your
    belt,
Toenails painted crimson, lipstick too, like the ass of a certain ba-
    boon I knew.

You opened your blouse, urged me to take suck. Talk about blind
　　macaque luck!
Oh, it was heaven, heaven past eleven, there in the shade of the
　　tuq-tuq.

Know what? She was almost like me, but human and seldom found
　　up trees.
She just kept on nodding as I spoke—or jibber-jibber-jabber'd, no
　　matter.
What a marvel, the mess of riffs, tales&compleynt that spilled forth.
Then because or in spite of, perhaps even by custom, she lifted her
　　skirts
and proffered unto me—*mercy*—the loveliest basket of warm
　　desserts.

A-monk-a-monk-a-mee, a-monk-a-monk-a-yoo
I once knew a lady wot lived in a shoe
Had so many laces she didn't know wot to do
So many laces, faces, places . . . Wot's a girl to do?

I jibber-jabber'd, jibber-jibber-jabber'd myself to a proper lather
and whipped that lather into a nice thick batter and baked up a
　　waffle for you.

A-monk-a-mee-a-monk-a-yoo, I baked up a waffle for yoo
A-monk-a-mee-a-monk-a-yoo-a-monk-a-weeee

did "The Itch," "The Scratch," "The Scrunch," "The Shimmy,"
first at the Macombo, then Bisquick Jimmy's,
danced us some "Buzz Step" at the Du Drop till 4,
slipped back into gear, closed down Pete's Notorious Zanzibar.
Come dawn I played "You the Foo" on air-guitar.
You shrieked, you coo'd: I was your macaque megastar.
I filled your head with jungle lore. "Salawesi Baby Boy,
says you, "tell me, tell me, tell me some more!"

I once knew a lady who lived in a shoe
Had so many laces, eyelets, tassels, hassles, faces to see, places to be . . .
Wot, oh, wot's a girl to do?

Now I'm back in my tuq-tuq tree, where, you might say, I was meant
    to be.
Every so often I try to be human—
Right time, right place, right face—
then forget myself once I get to groovin'.
Thing is, what I most need to remember,
got to scurry on back up lest there's a change in the weather.

But know what? DO YOU KNOW WHAT?
I'm having such a ball, never ever do quite manage to get my act
    together.

A-monk-a-monk-a-mee-a-monk-a-monk-a-yoo

Get my ass caught out in the rain, all hell breaks loose.

Fur gets so damn wet and funky, can't hardly move.

Critter red alert!—might as well be stuck in a tub of glue.

I get bit. I get stung. Pretty momma's gone back to wherever
 she's from.

It's a long, long way back up, bloodied and beat.

I'm hanging out with the flying squirrels from now on, believe
 you me.

SELF-CRITICISM AT 3 A.M.

Don't take that call:
Deft veronicas in an empty stadium,
The wind's applause ardent but fitful.

CLOSING IT DOWN
ON THE PALISADES

I. SEPTEMBER

Kettles, rain hats—
the small, unopened bottle of Angostura bitters,
its label stained and faded with the years.

The breeze is doing something in the leaves
it hasn't been, not at this hour.
The light, as well.

Early yet for the cicadas,
their gathering rush and ebb.
Too cool,
the sun not high enough.

A cardinal darting among the shadows
in back of the yard,

only at this hour
and again at dusk.

What is it so touching
about these tiny episodes of color
amidst the greenery and shadows,
now and at day's end,

that puts to rout all other sentiment?

II. OCTOBER

The garbage truck compactor is grinding
all 24 volumes of the *Encyclopædia Britannica,*
1945 Edition, including Index and Atlas,
along with apple cores, bed linen, ashtrays
and all that remains of an ailing begonia.

It is raining, not yet light. The wrens
will have put off their convening on the hemlock.
The distant beach homes of Malibu
come strangely to mind, high on the cliffs
overlooking the Pacific,

and how, now and then, after a terrible storm,
the soil beneath washes away, followed
not long after by the house itself, sliding
then crashing to the rocks below, its side tables,
vanities and clocks licked at

by the gathering foam and, finally, pulled to sea.
Every Saturday they awaken me before dawn,
lights flashing, men shouting, the hydraulic whine
of the compactor as it gnashes away:
desk drawers, yearbooks, sugar bowls.

I shall miss them. I shall miss
the sound of passenger jets overhead
making their descent into Newark in the rain,
before dawn, the first arrivals of the day,
with groggy visitors from Frankfurt, Bahrain.

There is hardly anything left to take—
lamps, a chair, bedspring and mattress.
The last roses still abloom out in the yard.
I can't tell you what kind, pink and white,
the tallest of them 6, 7 feet high.

Then, that'll be it till spring.
That'll be it till spring.

1975

Even the crickets are unnerving me tonight,
and the smell of camphor in the warm room
worse still; my woolens will outlast me.
Home again, from points north, west,
a suitcase full of useless books and no prospects.
There's a folk song that goes like that:
insipid—pathetic, really—without the music.
This appears to be a condition I shall not escape,
a gravitational field to be suffered through all my days,
like some wayward, doomed alien.
At least the folks are asleep. Getting along in years,
they shrug. A shrug means peace.
The stomach knows, when the clams are bad, or worse.
Perhaps that is truly the site for love,
or where love takes root, finally, and sets up shop.
I had imagined something much less uncomfortable.
The dirty aureole across the Hudson is New York.
Jets sink into it. Here, on the cliffs opposite,
trees whisk themselves. The wind freshens for rain.

Even George Washington, on the lam from Howe,
hid out here. He ate and ran
south. Ask any ghost along the Hackensack.
It's late, very late; that I do know.
Mother's bought new bed linen for the occasion,
described on the package as "duck egg blue,"
so clean and cool I could be afloat on a lake.

THE CROSSING

To carry this across, then,
like contraband from one country to another,
the hour before dawn:
this border outpost half-hidden beside a copse of laurel,
quiet for the moment, the guard asleep
or having headed home early, before the change in shift—
senior enough to get away with such things—
to slide back into bed beside his warm, sleeping wife.

A lamppost, the light flickering amidst the trees,
the mist still heavy . . .

Imagine what we're spiriting across as a large wooden tray,
one with a glass cover,
perhaps like those trays filled with butterfly specimens
one pulls from drawers in museums;

or, better still, moths, yes, moths,
floating in the tray like pieces of fabric,

that if touched would turn to dust on one's fingers;
or, if you like, a sheet of papyrus, ancient, discolored,
adorned in glyphs, like patterns in a Lepidoptera's wing,
floating atop a pool of solution,
kept together only by dint of the liquid's surface tension.

To carry you across
from the shadow country, with its multitudinous stairwells,
tiered rail stations and Victorian hotel lobbies
with their raft of private alcoves off to the side
into this harshly lit arena of insensate, bleating forms.

I am, as whenever we meet, overcome.
The tenderness and sorrow I feel in your presence
a kind of exquisitely sweet agony, unbearable nearly.

How can you pretend to be half a stranger
when we are brothers;
how can you stay away for many months, years on end,
only for us to meet up again like this
in one of these cloakrooms or pantries,
the voices, lit chandeliers and clatter in the drawing room next door,
with me beseeching you, as I always do.

Please stay,
you mustn't leave, not this time.

And you, eyes averted, looking cornered, confused . . .
Until you slip away once more,
retreating, like a wounded animal into the bush.

EXILES

The Super Chief speeds across the American West.
Herr Doktor Doktor Von Geist pulls the ends of his mustache,
almost like a seabird
maneuvering his wings in unsettled weather,
while he gazes out at the desolation and tumbleweed—
the *echo-less-ness*, as that bore Krenek likes to put it—
moon drifting in and out of the clouds.
With a formal solemnity, confused, perhaps with dignity,
along with the deliberateness of a surgeon,
he runs his fork through the orange emulsion
covering his salad,

        or what they call here salad.
—*Anything wrong, sir?* asks the black waiter,
who, the Doktor notes,
bears more than a passing resemblance to Louis Jordan;
that would be Louis Jordan of jump band fame,
not the other.

Door ajar to the great actress's cabana at Nazimova's Garden of Allah,
she lies back on her chaise longue,
gently running a finger along her glistening auburn lanugo,
while, at the same time, changing stations on the radio
until she arrives at *Amos and Andy*, her favorite:
   —*Holy Mackerel, dere, Andy!*
—*Ha, ha, ha, ummmmm,* die Schwarzen . . .
Just then, Tadzio walks past,
angelic boy in his sailor suit, right off the page,
the *plage*, still shaking sand off,
and catches a glimpse of Frau Lola,
pleasuring herself in anticipation of a visit from Salkia,
or the English tennis star, or, God forbid, Harpo.
But no, it is Tadzio, lovely Tadzio,
who neither blushes nor even seems taken aback.
—*Möchten Sie Pussy essen?*
she asks in a childish voice.
                              —*Schmeckt gut . . .*
But the boy's German is imperfect.
Besides which, he has plans for the afternoon.

The second, or is it the third, Mrs. H.,

consort of the distinguished foreign character actor,

wrinkles her nose,

as if downwind from a giant log of baking Liederkranz.

From high on a stage of his own imagining,

and looking out upon the *mausoleum of easy going*,

the Revolutionary Playwright

in his tailored denim Worker's costume

loads up and begins cranking away,

the Gatling Gun of Wilshire Boulevard:

Francis Assisi at an aquarium

Chrysanthemums in a coal mine

Lenin at the Prater

Tahiti in Metropolitan Form

—*Are we done yet, darling?*

she asks, slowly removing her husband's hand

from the smoking weapon.

Nietzsche, playing his second shot
on the dogleg par 5 eighth at Bel-Air,
shanks it into the creek.
                              —You are a great man,
Freddy, my boy, a great, great man,
his celebrated playing partner, the misanthropic jokester, intones.
The philosopher stands there, motionless, stricken,
his muttonchops and jowls sinking into the collar
of his powder-blue dacron golf shirt:
dismay, terror, puzzlement, the call of an unfamiliar bird?
                              —No great tragedy,
Herr Schickelgruber, a mere bump in the road, bump in the road,
knocking a bee off his plus fours with an antique mashie.

HOLLYHOCKS IN THE FOG

Every evening smoke blows in from the sea,
sea smoke, ghost vapor
of lost frigates, sunken destroyers.
It hangs over the eucalyptus grove,
cancels the hills,
curls around garbage sacks outside the lesbian bar.

And every evening the black bus arrives,
the black *Information* bus from down the Peninsula,
unloading the workers at the foot of the block.
They wander off, this way and that, into the fog.
Young, impassive, islanded within their tunes:
Death Cab for Cutie, Arcade Fire . . .

From this distance they seem almost suspended,
extirpated, floating creatures of exile,
as they walk past the Victorian facades
and hollyhocks in their fenced-in plots,
red   purple   apricot
solitary as widows or disgraced metaphysicians.

Perhaps they're exhausted, overwhelmed by it all:

spidering the endless key words, web pages,

appetite feeding on itself:

frantic genealogists, like swarms of killer bees.

The countless, urgent inquiries:

the poor *Cathars* and the *Siege of Carcassone*—

what can these long-ago misfortunes tell us of ourselves, of life—

Epinephrine-induced response,

Ryne Duren + wild pitches + 1958 . . .

Knowledge a trembling Himalayas of rubble:

Huitzilopochtli, Chubby Checker . . .

But for now they are done, till the bus comes again tomorrow.

There is nothing further to be known.

The fog, like that animate *nothingness*

of Lao-Tzu's sacred Tao,

has taken over the world, and with night settling in,

all that had been, has ever been, is gone,

gone but for the sound of the wind.

HOOTIE BILL DO POLONIUS

T-bone rare
And a side of brain stir-fried

Is how we liked it
And that's how it'd come out

The both *t*'s crossed, *eyes* dotted
And bloody in between

The weather that season was *puhfect*
Or most nearly so

As for the sun
You could make for the foliage

Or no
We was thoroughly rich and young

And the ladies legs
Kept on

And on and on and on
Like Texas

Sonnyboy
We *pre-ZIDED* over that patch of dust

Knew it
And *wore* it as befits self-knowledge

What queered it in the end
Was what the Right Reverend calls *puce-salami-tea*

Can't spell it
Don't know how to say it right

But know what it means
And what it means is *adios compadre*

To a most galuptious scene Kid
Very

RAIN

I

The room darkens,
then darkens further with the approach
of yet another storm cell from the west
with its columns and plaits,
the tall, ghostly chambers of space between—
une fraction intense de météore pur . . . —
willow, sage, Sung green, a hint, perhaps, of Veronese;
now darkening further still
until sufficiently dark, as if at the beginning of a show,
and with the sound of it the only sound.
At which point, and not before,
might one begin to detect his outline in the rain,
like an image hidden in a picture puzzle,
slipping about, darting like a pike,
over the hoods and under the chassis of parked cars,
making an appearance in the branches
of this tree or that: immaterial, flowing, wraith-like.

His fur now Grisaille, now Old Holland, then mouse,
altering in hue, just as the rain itself amidst its own shadows,
finally becoming one with the rain, and vanishing.

II

M. Francis Ponge, exemplar of phenomenology
and the breathing of *things*,
is sitting in the unlit front room, drapes pulled,
solemnly rapt, in the manner of a fascinated child
at home from school with the grippe.
In the distant background Señor Mompou is working through
a few sonorities —
La sonnerie au sol des filets verticaux . . .
M. Ponge is watching the entirety of Warner Bros.' *Looney Tunes*,
Vols. I and *II*, over and over, for hours on end,
while outside the rain continues to pour down.
The splashes of green, red and yellow
jump from the screen into the darkness of the room,
attended by a battery of sound effects
mixed in with splattered chestnuts from the Romantic age.
His English is very good, impeccable, really,
but these bursts of imprecation, muttered aside,
the minatory soliloquies; these somehow defeat him utterly.

Still, his absorption is not unlike that of a scientist
examining cells which behave oddly under the microscope,
and likewise mirthless, amidst an assault of mirth.
Daffy, Tweetie Bird, Yosemite Sam—
each of them intriguing, but Bugs, Bugs Bunny,
having quite a time of it out there on the other side of the curtain,
is who most commands the attention of M. Ponge,
lapsed surrealist, champion of the apple
in all it apple-ness, and so on.
Is it the "wascally wabbit's" outsize incisors?
The rain-colored fur with its white piping?
His buoyant cruelty and its inventive expression?
The resourcefulness, the abrupt sentiment?
It is, I tell you, all of these things, and more,
more than you or I have the capacity to imagine,
resolving themselves into that one "sensitive chord,"
which may one day come to be a *text* entitled "Bugs."

SNOW

The tank column moves east in the snow.
You cannot hear them at this remove,
High above and at an oblique angle:
The "bird's-eye view," much favored by mapmakers.
There are no birds, long gone to the south.
The sky is empty and will remain so for months,
Excepting attack planes and bombers,
Nowhere in evidence this evening. Nothing aloft
In this weather. The tanks continue on,
Covering great distances across the snow-covered grasslands,
Loath to stop lest their engines seize up in the cold.
The tessellations of tank treads vanish nearly as soon
As they are made. Nothing blocks the way ahead.
Nothing is gaining upon them from behind.
Their turrets judder in the fierce cross-winds.
This is a lacuna, whiteness, between what was
And what is about to become, in countless volumes,
In rack upon rack of grainy newsreel footage, history.

Flanked by Chevaux-Légers Lancers
In slate blue tunics with crimson facing
And a squadron of Neapolitans,
Resplendent in sky blue and yellow parade costumes,
Led by Prince Rocco della Romano
Known, among the ladies of Vilna, as Apollo Belvedere,

The Imperial Convoy sets off in the night,
The Emperor swaddled in bear furs
And alongside him the Duc de Vicence, Caulaincourt,
Recording the great man's every observation.

Behind, following in three sleds, the Grand Marshal,
Grand Equerry and Count Lobau,
And, riding horseback alongside, hard by the first sled,
Roustan, Imperial Mameluke, and Wonsowicz,
Brought along to translate into Polish.
Racing on past Vilna, shedding men and horses,
Picking up replacements along the way,
The convoy speeds across the icy wastes,
Outrunning the Cossacks, turning left
At Neman Bridge, their store of wine bottles
Exploding as they go, each like a pistol's report,
They arrive at the Tuileries in just two weeks,
Before midnight, and bearing news.

And far to the east, under the ice
And snow, at the bottom of Lake Semlovo,
Abandoned on the retreat from Smolensk,
Almost the entire treasure of Muscovy:
Porcelain, amber, jasper from the Urals,
Candelabras in the Japanese style,
Samovars, armor, silverware,
Along with the little precious things:
Enamel *kovshi*, snuff and powder boxes,
Bracelets, earrings, amulets—
Of every kind, so numerous
And of such a value as to be beyond reckoning.

EPISTLE XXXIX

Aggrievius, how is it I'm certain that you, no other,
will be the one to speak most eloquently at my memorial?
Because it is you, dear friend, who best husbanded
kind remarks of any sort, and, likewise, praise, in life,
the better that it might gush forth now in a single, extravagant go.
There you are, struggling, fighting back your grief. It's evident
to everyone on hand: the strangled, staccato bursts,
the troubled breathing. Hang in there, old son, you've rehearsed
too long and hard to get tangled up in sentiment now.
There, there, you're beginning to calm down. We're all relieved,
even me, and I'm dead. Behold, Aggrievius, in full sail,
canvas snapping in the wind as we approach his peroration.
It's true, you know, I really was a decent chap, underneath:
kind to dogs, shop clerks—and something of a wit, to boot.
You trot out a few of my *bons mots* to make that very point, suggesting
that my more fierce or pungent asides are better left shelved
for now. —*Ho,ho, ho*, the assembled murmur, demurely.
A few of the best were at your expense, but we'll let that go.
You would have filed in, the lot of you, to Biber's *Rosary Sonatas,*

the Crucifixion part, "Agony in the Garden," all that.

Hardly the soundtrack, one would have guessed, for an old, dead Jew.

Quite a few of these chicks on hand have it going on still, eh?

You'd really have to blow it big time not to get laid,

what with all the tears, perfume, black lace . . . Am I being awful?

Forgive me. But it is my party, after all. *After all*, after all.

I'd say, on balance, it was a very nice show. In fact,

I might as well have scripted it myself, perhaps with better pacing.

But I could not have improved upon your speech, Aggrievius, no.

It really is you, finally, who knew me best and loathed me most.

THE EXQUISITE ATMOGRAPHY OF THOMAS APPLETREE, DIARIST OF EDGIOCK

And thus did the Atmospherical Theatre play out,
with its transmutations & shifting of vapours,
whether the rain-bearing clouds of January
riding over our heades like vast Carracks
or Bulging, dull-swelling Bas-Relieve clouds
bloated & pendulous, *ubera caeli fecunda*:
sky cubbies or udders clouds;
Enclosed & stufft ye whole visible Hemisphere
in colour like Lead-vapours
or a tall Frescoo ceiling, or marbled veined grotto.

All symphonicall to my Genius,
regaling my cloud-born, my Nubigenous Genius,
Black clouds, gross & mineral fumes
vomited out of a Cupella;

Aeriall nitre, black lists,
Clouds heaped in cliffs, dreadfull & vast;
and winds, violent & furious
so as to Rock the Turret until I could not write,
and with the candle dancing & waving
hardly see, whilst the obstinate cold
did pinch my fingers;

until the Heavens, having discharg'd the ore-glutted Rain,
Rain of the Gulf, bosom & vagina of the Sea,
the Recesses, cu—nt or Rima magna,
having emptied their Lax fluid,
take on the Form of airy-marble.

And later next day my inkpot thawed.

Those Medicelestiall seas of Atmosphere,
a Mappa Mundi depeinted in clouds.

Language is exceeding scanty & barren
for apt similes & termes.
I tire myself with Pumping.
More fruitfull than all the King's tongues,
She is infinite & large,
they only a combination of sounds

from changes of Letters 24;
wich is easily computed, but Her inventory shop
& Particulars of her grand warehouse
are above ye Rules of Arithmetic.

So when those atoms of air invade my pores,
settling the fibres of my brain, ideas even,
an agreeable misty rain in spring
becomes a soothing anodyne to my vexations,
falling in patt with my humour,
a distillation, divine juice, Lachrymall Serentity;

BALSAMIC PANSPERMICAL PANACEA JUICE OF HEAVEN

Every vegetable strutted in vivid new-fed green,
Swelled & distended with ye vernal success,
Semole breasts of youthful lust;

Sanative steams, cordiall odours,
a fragrancy on my clothes ;
[the year's first butterfly (4 May)]

a nutrimental teeming influence,
as frogs=spawn or jelly or sperma ceti;
dropping in unseen effluvia,

efflorescence & unctuous irrigation,
ye Reall muck of the air,
Rich magazine of Aerial dispensary,
aura vitalis on earth's longing womb.

How ye may draw all ye Bedlam whims,
this region of chimeras,
cities, armies, whatever ye teeming imagination suggest
in this the Book, the Grand history
& Picture of mine own life,
which is same as the Sky over Edgiock.

Composed from entries in the 1703 weather diaries of Thomas Apple-
tree, the presumed Edgiock Diarist, transcribed by the scholar Jan Golin-
ski from the Lancing College Archives, Lancing, West Sussex

TO MY CAT WILLIAM

Mr. Boo, be still
It's 3 a.m.
Furhead simulacrum of my restive heart
You do, you do, you do as you will

Bother, bother
. . . Poppa, Poppa!
Transformado en mi gato
Oh, mi Dios
The things night brings us
Am I dreaming
Are you really you, or you

Companion on this distressed plot
Your wakefulness, health
Mine not
The broken-up bits of me
Scattered, shivering like mercury

Tickletickle

Pother, pother

Willie Nocturne's now my father

Hullo, Poppa

Hullo, Sonny

Say, wasn't that you I saw in the funnies

Mr. Bissou

It's so late, Boo

Willie Nocturne

Now it's your turn

Off you go, then

I'm your father

N-O, that spells no, sir

Oh but oh but oh my heart so

Sore is, Poppa

Sore

MY LIFE IN LETTERS

There you are,
looking like the Khan's most favored concubine,
but in a London doorway,
cigarette and beige Aquascutum, smiling,
at me, it would seem,
all ardor, woundedness and hope.
How would I not have adored you?
And you . . . and you . . .
"Dear August . . ." Oh, no I can't, please . . .
The carnage . . .

Drifts of blue aerogrammes:
I tried phoning last night . . .

If I could somehow make a single balloon payment
to rid myself of all this,
or with a click, like Adobe Reader downloads:
Clear List

Worse still the weight of kindness—
tumuli, drumlins, lava heaps of kindness,
everywhere, choking the landscape . . .

Must I just now be reminded:
how much, how often, how many, and unprompted?

Dare I pretend to be worthy?
I would be a monster.
Monster? you say.
Please, I am too inconsequential . . .

I'm sorry, I'm sorry . . .
STOP IT, WITH THE "I'M SORRY," DAMMIT!

No, no, I have disappointed everyone.
Even those of you who might have believed otherwise,
trust me, you were mistaken.

40 years, 20 marbled letter files of proof:
I stand here before you, the accused.

WHEN THE BAROCCO

When the Barocco
came over the hill with its cerulean vaults and golden exhortations
Otto in the tower took leave of his *Fleisch*,
attending to the rumble in the near beyond.

Up the staircase of the Dolomites
and along the length of the turquoise river,
streaming in channels of differing hue,
it bounded like a beach ball across the great passes,

the summer pastures,
flattening all that came before it,
down the slopes,
through woodland and paddock,

coming to rest
but a furlong from the thornèd hedge
of Otto and his forbears' village,
and there, sweating dew,

matted with pine needles, grape mash,
insects, rodents, all manner of grasses,
like a vast, lopsided globe,
opalescent, trembling,

a planet unto itself,
very like a planet, there it sat,
a colossus, a visitation,
blocking what remained of the afternoon light

and emitting a kind of tuneful bleating,
2 parts piccolo, one, perhaps, trombone.
A most remarkable phenomenon to behold.
The villagers trembled from behind mud walls.

Otto thence convened the Elders.
The alphorn was taken up and blown,
first a necklace of quarter notes, then one long,
and from the forests all around,

like fleas off a hound,
came the Woodwoses from their rustic nests,
a swarm of hairy Calibans,
waving pointed sticks,

chisels, flints, hatchets and cudgels,
and fell upon it,
poking and flailing. You'd have thought
it was just a big *piñata*.

While from inside came an ominous strange music:
first, a silvery harmonic fuzz,
then some spectral pedal tones
that suggested the tolling of bells,

then an agitated chromaticism, then . . .
then . . . o, dear, then . . . . . .
Like lava from deep in a seething volcano
out burst a geyser of foam,

a foam of stucco and plaster,
covering butcher-yard and meadow, orchard and cow path,
pigs at their acorns,
hares, bears and Hans,

dozing behind the refectory,
Churrigueresque, like whipped cream,
suddenly dripping off half-timbered houses,
the town hall and chapel,

their corpses stacked high like cordwood
dead Styrians and Savoyards,
and that doyen among rivers, the Enns,
for no good reason o'erflowing its banks,

and Otto, Otto the pious, spellbound:
ovals, porticos, diagonals, whorls,
staircases, credenzas, putti galore.
Wine ran like squirrels in the forest.

And down from the sky above
fell ribands of damask, of silk, then a fine rain,
more a mist,
colored purple in patches, or ochre, indigo or gold,

inlaying plain gardens with mother-of-pearl.
Pageants sprouted like mushrooms.
Trompe l'oeil windows opened room upon room,
and in the trees passacaglias

of birdsong. Not a birch
nor gable left unfestooned, the valley
awash in high color
and upon itself enfolding, trebly enfolding,

until what had been *there*, *there*,
and *there*, earthbound, fixed in repose,
all now in concert reaching heavenward
moved.

SPORTS WRAP

Who would have credited their late August collapse?
They flourish like jumpweed over these punishing summers,
or did do, adversaries going faint here alongside the river.
Eighteen-wheelers bust across the interstates, devouring horizon,
tuned to the one same station, signal fluttering
as this distressing tale unfolds, inning by inning, game by game.

Do you suppose, in the beginning, there was an actual Denny
for whom the tuna melts, iced tea and assorted sides
were meant as commemorative, an act of devotion?
Surely someone has written on this subject at length.
But is it not pleasing to think of a corporeal Denny—
adored child, doting granny, down-home, deep-dish Salomé—

living in one of those clapboard shitholes behind a silo,
playing at quoits, kibitzing, shrieking like an infidel set alight?
            —*Skip, you must be as baffled as anyone.*
The veteran field general gazes into the near distance.
You know this look: cerebral, resolute—contempt?—
big hair threatening to erupt from under his cap.

The cell is vibrating in his left front pants pocket:
three likelihoods, none of them at this moment inviting.
Who attends to these staged postmortems on TV:
inebriates, the eviscerati, Denny, you, me?

       —I wish I knew the answer to that one,
Pete. I do. I really, truly do.

SUMMER JOURNAL

[3 P.M.]

Loss leaders in shop windows,
fog spilling down the slopes
of Corona Heights, Twin Peaks, Tank Hill—

my name on everyone's lips:

—*August*, they say,
with resignation and dismay,
pulling up their collars against the wind.

[BLUE]

The student doctors in blue scrubs,
passing up and down Parnassus to the hospital,
now invisible, on top of the hill,

past the bougainvilleas and kebab shop:

18-, 30-hour shifts, back and forth,
out on their feet, ghostly in the fog.

"Coming Up the Hudson,"
the altered title of an old Monk tune —

why, when the interns and residents drift by,
must it be these particular words that assemble in my mind?

[L'ART POÉTIQUE]

—Just let it sit there for a while cooking in its own juices,

my father used to say
of a dish newly taken hot from the oven.

[GARDEN OUT BACK WINDOW]

White, the jasmine and magnolia,
set off by the dark green shellac of its leaves;
red, the trumpet vine winding up the palm,

fuchsia and tequila sage;
the orange nasturtium flower, marmalade bush
in flame;
and Hooker's evening primrose:

the sphinx moth at dusk, the hummingbird
dipping into its nectar wells,
the goldfinch visiting for its black seeds;
bright yellow,
the color heightened in gray light—

neon along the fogbound Ginza.

[MAP]

On the wall of the darkened hallway,
not long before dawn,
horns baying out by the rocks
muffled by fog—
"All Blues" played through a Harmon mute . . .

Europa, the wild dog,
her snout in the Pyrenees, licks clean

the Gouffre de la Pierre St. Martin
below the Pic d'Arles,

knocking sideways the steeples
of Zaragoza,

then slobbering into the Río Jalón.

[GOLDEN GATE]

Two turkey vultures, wings unfurled like spinnakers,
dry and groom themselves,
late morning atop Yellow Bluff.

The decks of the bridge vibrate:
El Caminos, Acuras, Cabriolets—

within their plastic and metal housings,
sentient beings,

in whose own housings, brain pans and soft tissue,
imaginings, dreams, the phantom conversations
are played and replayed.

Diadems, crab mites, worm larvae in the Bay below . . .

—*Subhuti, are there many particles of dust*
in the 3,000 chiliocosms?

—*Very many, World-Honored One.*

[TUESDAY]

The same, and the same again . . .

The oboist upstairs—
why does he insist on practicing during my afternoon nap?

Why does it always have to be Ravel?

[SNOWY PLOVER]

Snowy plovers
hopping this way and that in the wet sand,

skirmishing, posturing, poking around for bugs.

The vast, bruise-colored fogbank
sitting out there,
spread across the horizon like some dreadful prophecy
waiting to blow in.

New York, London—
a great busy-ness and agitation in the streets,
offices, gathering places

among those who truly matter,
assembling that day's world, disassembling it,
commenting at length on same.

[CLOUD FOREST]

I took him up to the Cloud Forest,
just behind the Medical Center.
Snails crunched in the soft duff underfoot.
This upset him.
Water dripping from the eucalyptus:
the sharp tap-tap of a downy woodpecker,
its sound reverberating among the treetops.

Ischi, Issa, Issa, Ischi.

Try saying that ten times fast as you can.
The haiku master in his quilted priest robes,
the "last wild Indian" in his bark knickers.
They took a good, long look at each other.
Actually, they could well have passed for brothers,
the heathen fitter and darker
by several shades. Gentle sorts, the two of them,
and taciturn as can be. No harm there;
not like an Algonquin Round Table was on tap.

Can't really say what I reckoned was on tap.
Ischi, since they first smoked him out,
behind the slaughterhouse over in Oroville,
this is now his place, his home.
Every so often they come up the hill and fetch him:
some big shot out-of-town phrenologist
wanting to whip out the calipers, poke him, make him say *ahhh*.
Otherwise, they leave him be,
happy as Larry with his grubs and chipmunks and handicrafts.

Issa much taken with the yellow banana slugs:
Readers will well know how he feels about gastropods,
54 haiku devoted to the snail alone.

The two of them seem to be hitting it off,
in their quiet way, just sitting there on a log,
the one whittling away, the other staring at the ground.
Don't even seem aware that I'm around.

[DEAD ZONE]

The *dead zone*—

headlights catch the fog pooling round the tires
of oncoming traffic.

All-Star break, midsummer,
football still 8 weeks away:
you hear it in the voice of the radio sports talk host,

the pitch half an octave higher,
the rush of words, the combativeness,
no one calling in but the hard cases,

the same sad, old bachelors,
chewing the cud, chewing the cud, chewing . . .

[WIND/WORK]

The sound of the wind awakens me,
I cannot say what time,
but in the depths of night.
I can tell by the absence of street noise.

The gusts seem to arrive in sequences of three,
two short, one long—
violent anapests, the last the most protracted
and fierce,
gaining in force over its duration,
tossing the big palm's crown of fronds
until they crackle,
bending back the top of its trunk.
The building itself trembles.

Then a few minutes of calm until the next rush
of wind, each sequence more intense
than the last until it finally blows itself out.

I lie there struggling to remember a word.
It takes a while,
but it's not far. As I begin to doze off
it comes to me,
as so many things do in this condition of mind.

Zamboni

Just the word,
not the ice-restoring machine of hockey arenas,
or Mr. Zamboni of Paramount, California,
and his ungainly, lucrative invention.

It was necessary that I find the word.
Whatever else happens in the course of the day,
the important work has been done.

[CABINET OF TIMBRES]

From my Cabinet of Timbres
I remove two viols, one treble, one bass, a theorbo,
chitarrone, violin and, bless her,
here comes Ludmilla from the front room
wheeling the chamber organ down the hall.

I draw my bath,
as I do every morning this time of year
with the world outside having disappeared
but for the greenery out back, foregrounded,
bobbing and trembling in the stiff sea wind.

I shall have my chord,
even if I have to sit here soaking in this dark room
the entire morning.

                   Schmelzer, Biber, Kapsberger—
it's in there somewhere

among the toccatas, sonatas, chaconnes.
I know because I have heard it there before.

HOW MANY TIMES

Master claps of thunder,
Wrath of God thunder—
Sitting on the porch at night and waiting
For the rain to fall in Texas;

Or at the Cantina Grill Express
In Denver airport, between flights,
Watching as you dab at some hot sauce
On your chin:

How many times, how many places,
Have I said "I love you"?
How many _____ does it take
To change a lightbulb?

Watching smoke from the sugar beet plant
Drift east to Minnesota
From the hotel window in Fargo—
How many times "You are beautiful"?

The swami,
After an extended meditation
In his hut, in the pine forest,
Many kilometers distant

From the nearest village
And at an altitude
From which one can see
Not only that village, but the next

And the next,
Takes out a cigarette,
Lights it,
And inhales deeply.

ROSE EXILE

The parade floats trundle north along South Orange
in the clammy darkness and floral decay of pre-dawn Pasadena,
turning right onto the long stretch of Colorado Boulevard,
following exactly the parade route of the celebrated Tournament
    of Roses.

Burbling from speakers hidden in the palms and sycamores
one can, just, make out the *aching majesty* of Richard Wagner's
Siegfried Idyll and *Rhine Journey*, Furtwangler—who else—
conducting the Wiener Philharmoniker.

First, in perfect scale, bright vinyl fringe bedecking the bottom,
a bungalow-sized replica of the Vienna Court Opera,
is followed by yet another float, the Café Griensteidl, also from
    "Old Wien,"
with its Jugendstil lamps and marble-topped tables.

A local bit player, having grown out his sideburns,
solemnly writes down notes on a stave, while nibbling a Sacher torte:

Richard Strauss, let us say, at work on an opera.
And what are we now to think of Richard Strauss?

Following next, on a platform atop a huge frankfurter float,
comes the co-author of the *Dialectic of Enlightenment*,
seated behind a desk and clapping his hands to his ears
in a mechanical fashion, not unlike a windup toy.

This is not the desk later memorialized on Adorno-Platz in
    Bockenheim
but the desk from his Brentwood home at 316 South Kenter
(just a few doors down from the O.J. unpleasantness years later),
the tall, elaborate Bismarck-era monstrosity

with its multitude of small drawers and, beside it, the carved
    wooden chair
on which the great man now sits, in extreme agitation, crying out:
"Wo ist die Aura? Wo ist die Aura?"
The source of his distress is standing directly to his right

in a form-fitting sequined gown, singing in a voice one critic
    described as:
"trumpet-clean," "pennywhistle piercing," "Wurlitzer wonderful."
You will know of whom I'm speaking.
It is the "brass diva" herself, Miss Ethel Merman,

belting out a hair-raising version of "I Get a Kick Out of You."

"What's with the long face, Pudge," she growls,

realizing she will not, has not, moved Wiesengrund-Adorno, not
one eeny-weeny bit.

"Loosen up and live a little, Mr. Big Shot Wisenheimer."

At this moment bombers are assembling into their formations over
Europe.

Dishes on their rubber racks are almost now completely dry.

Someone is inventing color TV.

Millions of cans of corn niblets sit in the darkness on shelves
across the Midwest.

The streets remain empty.

The circumstances had been made clear to the participants at the
start.

Trucks rumble in the distance across the Arroyo Seco,

while the first birds of the day, unbothered as ever, commence
their singing.

A HISTORY OF WESTERN MUSIC: CHAPTER 44

(BEBOP)

YAHTZEE   *YAHTZEE*   *YAHTZEE*

At Rapunzel's Fungible Ball
The most glittery jittery gala of all

The Vedettes & Babettes
Scarfed down crêpe suzettes
Orange butter spray-painting the walls

What a feast, what a fete
Scamps vamping away till last call

YAHTZEE   *YAHTZEE*

HIPPITY-HOPSIE

Strambunzella's combustible tattersall
A headache to even recall
So much effervescing Buzette lost first her *courgette*
Her silver barrette
Her earrings next you might say
Her bearings wobbling as if ready to . . .

At Rapunzel's jungle-y . . .
Even the discreet left their feet
Rapunzel's Fungible . . .

Varlots at the gate loath to wait
Tantrums broke plates—
A proper stromboli-strewn brawl

YAHTZEE   *YAHTZEE*

SWEET-DEW-DROPSIE

Quiddity's itch nay timidity's twitch toggle-switch bobble
Rob Pete to pay Gobble *tout de suite* move your feet try not to fall

YAHTZEE   YAHTZEE

REET PETITE-TATER-TOTSIE

A ramp'd up dance call it *cha-cha-faux-bocci*

CHOC-A-LATTA-CHOCK-A-LITA-CHOC-A-TIKKA-LOTTA

BOMBA-GA-BONGA-GA-BUM-GUM-
GA-HUBBLE-BUBBLE-SAMBA

STROMBOLITO ESCONDITO

AB-SOL-EET-LY TUTTI-FRUTTI

HAMMUROOBI

PEEK-A-BOOCHIE

SLOW-FAUX-BOCCI

Syncopated commotion   addled emu shunned

YAHTZEE   YAHTZEE   YAHTZEE

Rapunzel Rapunzel let down your . . .

The hottest ticket of all

Glittery Jittery

Rapunzel's Fungible Ball

WHEN THE FOG

When the fog burnt off that morning
Outsize JumboTron screens were hanging off the clouds,
Scores of them, huge, acres and acres of screen,
Shimmering.
Pixels the size of wagon wheels, damaged, flickering
Off and on, red, blue and green;
Faces, flags, county fairs—like pointillist cartoons,
Melting away, reconstituting:

Crowds, delirious crowds,
Waving drumsticks and banners—
Galvanically *us*,
Us whom we've been waiting for,
Smearing into vibrating puddles of color,
Then dissolving, like jet exhaust, into the air.

While outside the streets were empty.
Who is to say where everyone has gone?
Only the occasional sound truck, its barked entreaties

Too garbled to make out.

Then quiet.

Two scrub jays making a racket in the honey locust.

Sky darkening as weather gathers off the coast.

Quiet as an abandoned summer playhouse.

A WINE TALE

for Lee Harwood

Behind the chateau, its celebrated "candle-snuffer" towers
and Gothic traceries engraved and worn proudly on the labels
of how many bottles of pinot and Bourgogne,

the old caretaker sleeps in the shadow of the cistern, its wood
sweating and frayed, the autumnal, late-afternoon light
bringing to this rustic tableau
the kind of orange-tinted, unworldly radiance
he would remember from his childhood, viewing scenes
from *Snow White* and *Little Red Riding Hood* in the family attic,
having stolen off with his big sister's cherished stereoscope.

The depth and intricate plots of his dreams these past few weeks,
the harvest in and mornings darker by the day,
astonish him with their capacity for recall,
such a one as he would be hard-pressed to reproduce while waking:
the long-ago conversations, the detailed interiors

of that modest little house on the outskirts of the village,
not five kilometers from where he now lies,
awake and stunned by all that has taken place beneath his eyelids,
not to mention the emphatic *bande*
pitching a tent in the lap of his purple-stained coveralls.
Nearly 70, he thinks to himself, sheepish but rather pleased
at the impudence, the importunings of his valorous little friend.

He really mustn't drink so much with lunch anymore,
But there is so much of it at hand,
a beguiling vermilion and with that distinctive nose,
cherry, mint and leather, the tiered finish, in every swallow
the *goût de terroir*,
the smell of the earth after last night's rain,
the smell of all those Aprils and Septembers
here on the eastern slope of the Great Escarpment.

Who is to say if our friend is an epicure, a wastrel,
or but a simple man, a *paysan*,
of no particular ambition, wit or aptitude,
whose destiny has been to lift things up, clean them off,
and put them back down again where they belong
in paradise?

THE RAPTURE OF VACHEL LINDSAY

I am, Madam, no beggar, but a peddler of dreams,
Purveyor of the Gospel of Beauty, Reciter of Rhymes . . .

And they regarded him from the shadows of their porches,
country women: the "Sharecropper's Wife," "Woman of the High
    Plains,"
or their mothers. You've seen the photos.

What he wanted was a meal and kip for the night,
this feverish, one-man Chautauqua whose sweat brought to mind
the scent of yellow deer, and to deliver unto them exalted verse:
Poe, Milton, Swinburne, or his own "Laughing Bells," a standby,

or fairy stories, were there children on hand. There were.
And in return was served a plate of salt pork, more salt than pork,
a soup of cloudy, lukewarm water, tallow, wilted greens and half-
    raw biscuits.

And off he'd go again, as much as 40 miles in a single day,
200 miles in a single week,

sowing Beauty with his Rhymes, as Johnny Appleseed sowed orchards,
America-in-every-apple-Lindsay,
Lindsay of Springfield, Lincoln's Springfield,
with Campbellite fervor, the Immersionist's ardor,
warbling his canticles under the Church of Sky,
for Beauty and the Love of Jesus Christ, Our Savior, are as one.

Lindsay, Lindsay, more child than adult,
elemental as the Negro or Indian, all impulse&oratory,
from Mother&Springfield set forth
in his bowler hat, the better to catch cherries,
or his sombrero, to shield his face from the punishing sun,
oriflamme tie, yellow corduroys, an oilskin sack filled with Rhymes,
tremendous clouds overhead, interminable prairie stretching
     before him.

O, Florida . . .
Chaste Lindsay treading the *venereal soil*,
the primeval palm swamps and turpentine camps,
cassava and watermelon fields,
ever too late for dinner and down to his last few peanuts,
amidst the profusion of violets, turtles, snakes and cranes.

Stately, plump Waldo Scenery,
Delius playing on the old Victrola,
Adoze in his hammock 'midst the jungle greenery . . .

Hosts of bluebirds, the *lustrous bespangled ooze of swamps* . . .

Valdosta, Macon, whistling his way to Barnsville,

whistling through the night, crickets and bullfrogs,

washing up and doing his laundry under the falls at Tallulah,

waving to the chain gang outside Bobcat.

—*Now, son, answer me this: Does a nigger have a soul?*

Yes, Lindsay tells him.

—*Well, damn, you the first I ever hea' say so.*

Lake Toxaway, then the scarifying cliffs of Whiteside Mountain,

where he heard tell of a dog this one fella tied to an umbrella and
    let go.

Dog survived. The dog/man friendship no.

Highland, Cashier, Asheville . . .

Good barns and a *languid leanness among the men*

Slanderously attributed to the hookworm

And across the mountains to Tennessee,

the Seven Suspicions hard on his heels,

cross-logs bridging the streams, hills and scrub choking the horizon

as the slum buildings do in Chicago.

Lindsay picks a rose outside the town of Frog Pond,

among a sea of roses, just one, and sticks it in a jar upon a hill.

Sarsaparilla&Lemonade-Lindsay, St. Francis-of-the-Prairie-Lindsay,

marching from Springfield through Kansas, *BOOMLAY BOOM*,

like General William Booth Entering Heaven,
banjos, bass drums, tambourines going in his head all the time,
as he walked by the hedged fields and orchards,
through this landscape which above all others pleased him most,
on this *straight west-going road to the sunset,*
along the creeping Arkansas, its course marked by cottonwoods,
land green from yesterday's rain and the clouds above
patterning all before him like a carpet, BOOMLAY BOOM,
half-wild cattle grazing unbroken prairie sod
between alfalfa fields where hovered the lavender haze of fragrant
    blossom
and the busy music of gorging bumblebees,
Lindsay in his rapture, barking canticles under the Church of Sky,
waving wheat all around him, wheat the color of the sun,
clouds like continents above, prairie at his feet stretching on to
    eternity,
grain elevators disappearing behind him like ships in a geography
    book,
until the top of yet another begins to loom up in the west,
BOOMLAY BOOMLAY BOOMLAY BOOM,
helping himself to pulled taffy in an abandoned farmhouse,
the sweet song of the bird called the Rachel Jane
serenading him from a mulberry tree outside the loft window
of the barn where he'd been sleeping on alfalfa, *soft, fragrant&clean,*
eating wild strawberries on the way to Emporia,

riding into Pomona on a handcar, likewise to Wellsville, where he
  engaged in *picturesque talk*
with a handful of Mexicans,
trading his rhymes for breakfast in Cottonwood,
enjoying a good audience for his rhymes in Elondale,
nearly boo'd off the stage in Newton,
windmills turning, turning on a hill as he approached Spearville,
the barley slick and *fishy*, the oats *green&hairy*,
Lindsay, Lindsay, belonging to one of the leisure classes, that of the
  Rhymer,
dinner in *bang-up style* at the Sante Fe Station,
sends 10 dollars to Mother, buys 15 cents worth of figs in Cimarron,
barters Rhymes for a sandwich in Insalls,
where the druggist refused him ice cream in return for the same,
sitting down with the rest at Grant Wood's "Dinner for Threshers,"
caught up without warning in John Steuart Curry's "Spring
  Shower"–Lindsay,
all the while 'hoppers at him like hail, eating holes through his
  clothing.
BOOMLAY BOOMLAY BOOMLAY BOOM,
and along the road, to the one side of him touring cars with
  pennants:
Knox Roadsters, Otto Runabouts, a black Hupp-Yeats,
Chicago, New York, Emporia,

and to the other side, approaching on the creosote-soaked rail tracks,
all smoke and rackety fanfare—
The United States goes by! Lindsay writes in his notebook:

Listen to the iron horns, ripping, racking,
Listen to the wise-horn, desperate to advise-horn,
Listen to the fast-horn, kill-horn, blast-horn . . .

And this was the rapture of Vachel Lindsay,
Sarsaparilla&Lemonade-Lindsay, Momma's *petite-vache*-Lindsay,
those years before the Great War,
Greenwich-Village-to-Illinois-Lindsay, following the Allegheny,
crackers&cheese-Lindsay,
walking up and down Sixth Street in Los Angeles the
    whole-night-long-Lindsay,
composing the entirety of "General William Booth . . ." in his head,
standing on the shore of San Francisco Bay in despair,
ready to throw himself in, like Li Po into the Yang-tze, but sober.

Lindsay, Lindsay, Beauty in his left hip pocket,
chanting "Atalanta in Calydon" as he tramped through the Rockies,
trying to keep warm, and his favorite war cry, "Rah for Bryan!,"
all the while marveling at the "cyclorama,"
corduroys burst at the knee, sporting a red bandana . . .

"A very good boy," Robert Frost would say of him, "a kind of genius";
pausing a moment, "and just crazy."
Yeats taking in the spectacle of Lindsay on a visit to Chicago:
head thrown back, body tensed,
vibrating like a didgeridoo, arms pumping, up on the balls of his feet:
BOOMLAY BOOMLAY BOOMLAY BOOM.

These were the years after America had taken Lindsay to its heart,
this "prairie troubadour" with his "higher vaudeville":
colleges, high schools, ladies auxiliaries . . .
WHOOP WHOOP WHOOP–Lindsay,
with his golden *o*-sounds and hands aflutter in cornball *mudras* —
chanting away in that deep bass, the heavy accents very heavy,
then whispering, then changing tempo,
"an hour's intoxication," phrases "crashing through like college yells,"
"Pierrot with the paint removed from his face,"
"the most extraordinary embarrassment in our cultural history."

Lindsay, Lindsay, poor little calf . . .
You know, don't you, what America will do to you,
what truly befalls you should America take you to her heart . . .

Wendell Seeming is dancing, dancing on the roof of the Waldorf
*   Astoria*
in the Starlight Ballroom, and dancing very well.

There are big men who are light on their feet, you know.
And all that gin has made him lighter still. He very nearly floats.

Lindsay, Lindsay, in Pullmans, hotel rooms, packed auditoriums
from Brownsville to Bemidji, in flames, coming apart inside . . .
Poor little calf, good night.

TRAVELER'S TALES: CHAPTER 12

The cruise ship heads out of the harbor before dark
in the direction of Point Blanco and the sea beyond,
the din from the convent playground below having subsided
and the sickle moon making ready to take up its post
beside Venus and Jupiter, aligned this month,
and on display above the flood-lit cathedral.

They erupt like cicada whirr, like starlings
exploding from a tree at any sudden sharp sound,
dozens of three-year-olds in gray smocks
pouring from their captivity at end of day,
nuns chasing after them in their winged cornettes,
herding them the way border collies herd sheep.

The Mediterranean in four of your windows,
rose-colored stucco, green shutters, pan tile, clotheslines
trumpeting the Age of Cubism, as if for the first time.
You're well set-up, better even than on Point Grey Road:
English Bay, downtown lights, Grouse Mountain in that window
30 years ago. I turned up on your doorstep there, like this, as well.

And you on mine, troubled or jubilant or both.
It was a custom for Ming scholars to pronounce on friendship,
much given in their treatises to the notion of the *gaoshi*,
a virtuous and elevated Confucian sort of gent.
Whereas our discourse tends to run—well, think Hawaiian
coffee, but with a tilde over the *n* . . .

Puerile? Low? A couple of worthless graybeards
catching sunset from the balcony, sipping a noble tempranillo,
remembering: Are we not virtuous, as well?
For what, Li Zhiyan, is more virtuous than being in love,
carnal love, every lamp switched on in the Inner Kingdom,
tenderness radiating from every portal?

Does an Emperor in love freely choose to wage war,
or, unprompted, visit torment upon his own people?
On himself, perhaps, but that is another matter.
Friendship, too, is a kind of love, more lightly worn, enduring.
I read that in a book, and more than the one time.
Those who go on in such fashion might do better caulking or weeding.

You find yourself in the canals behind my forehead,
paddling. You do recall that particular mallard over there, yes?
And I in the high, rib-vaulted rooms your voice
rays out from itself, wherein I visit and take refreshment.
It has all turned out better than we probably dared hope.
It frightens me, just this moment, to say so.

ACKNOWLEDGMENTS

These poems first appeared in the following journals:
foam:e, London Review of Books, The New Republic, The New York Times, The Paris Review, Poetry Review.

"A Wine Tale" was printed as a broadside by the Woodland Pattern Book Center in Milwaukee.

The author wishes to thank the Lannan Foundation for its generosity and the *London Review of Books*, where all but a few of these poems first appeared.

Printed in the USA
CPSIA information can be obtained
at www.ICGtesting.com
LVHW091147150724
785511LV00005B/597